T0288404

Sticky Fingers and Night Flyers

CONTENTS

NATIONAL GEOGRAPHIC
School Publishing
Hampton-Brown

Blends with r, l

Look at each picture. Read the words.

Example:

frog

grass

truck

flag

plum

clock

High Frequency Words

- back
- body
- eat
- how
- into
- these
- those
- way

Key Words

Look at the pictures.
Read the sentences.

Frogs Are Fun!

1. Look at **these** frogs.
2. One has a little **body** and a red **back**.
3. **How** do they **eat**?
4. They grab bugs.
5. **Those** frogs hop **way** up **into** a tree.

Phonics Games
NGReach.com

Tree Frogs

by Barbara Wood

This is a tree frog. A tree is its home. It is a safe place to hide.

These are tree frogs, too.

Frogs Have Fingers

How can a frog cling to a tree? It has fingers with flat pads. The pads are sticky.

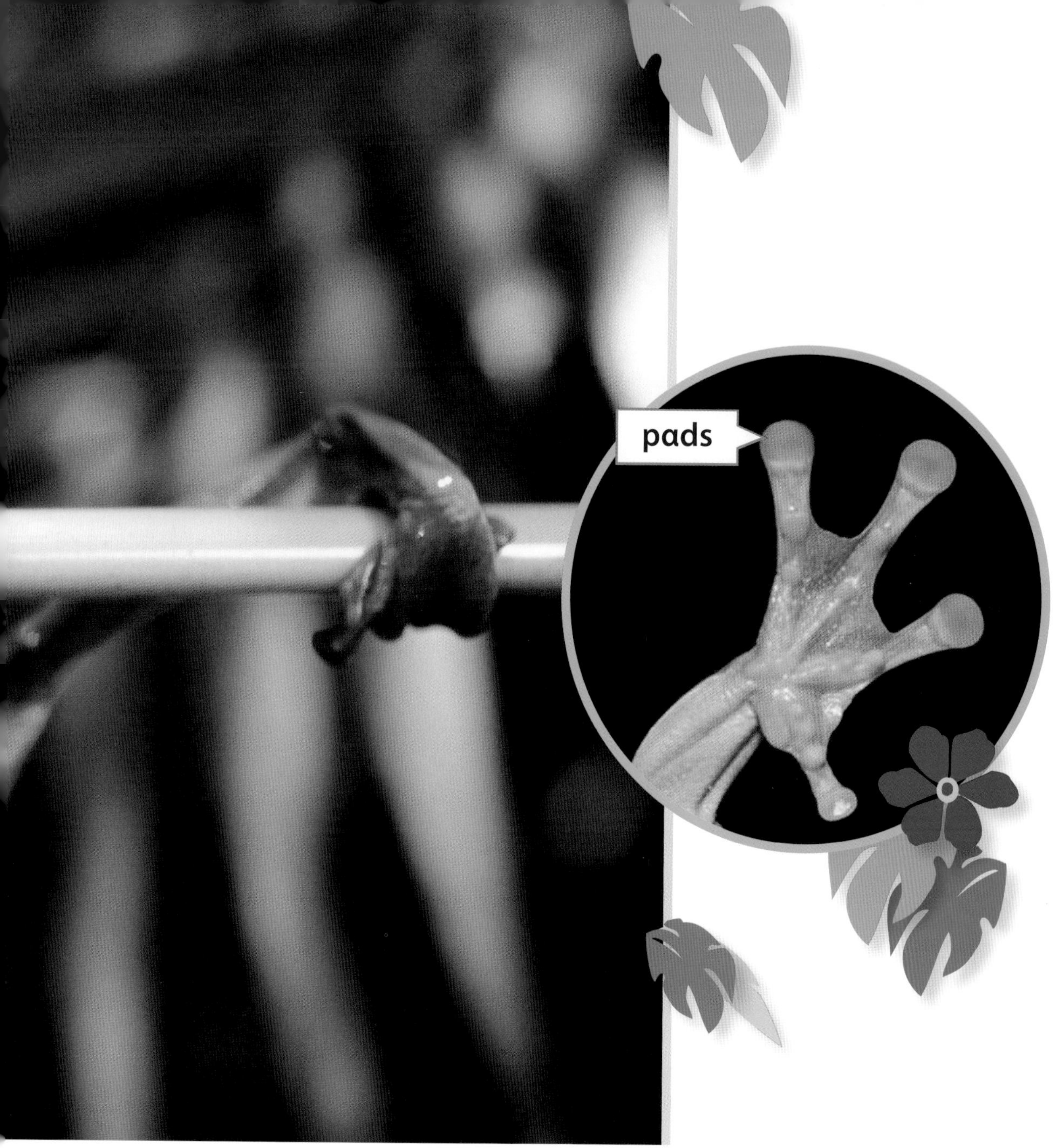

The pads help a frog grip. A frog can cling to a tree. It will not slip and drop.

Frogs Have Legs

This frog has a little body. But look at those long legs!

Long legs help frogs hop. They can hop from place to place. They can hop way up into trees.

Tadpoles

Look at the tadpoles! A tadpole will be a frog one day.

This little frog was a tadpole. It clings to the back of a big frog. When the big frog hops, it will not drop off. They can go way up into a tree.

Frogs Eat

Frogs eat bugs like these.

Look at the way this frog eats.
It grabs a bug. Frogs like to eat crickets.

It's a bit like we eat—without the bugs! ❖

Blends with r, l

Read these words.

grab	cling	bug	hop
grip	flat	drop	plum

Find words with **r** or **l** blends.
Use letters to build them.

g r a b

Talk Together

Choose words from the box above to tell a partner what a frog can do.

A frog can grab.

Blends with s

Look at each picture. Read the words.

Example:

stop

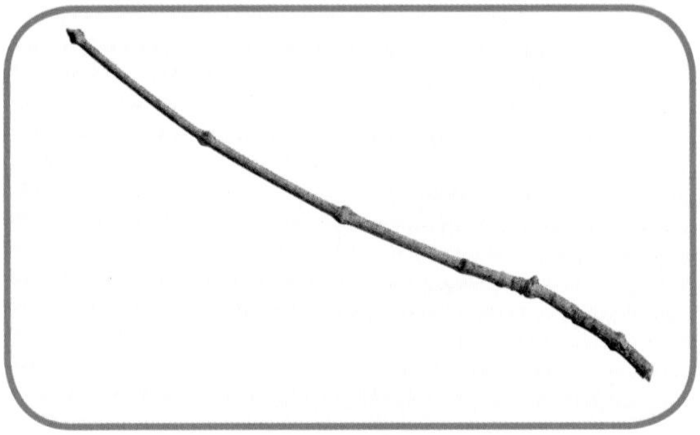

stick

spot

swim

stem

skip

High Frequency Words
back
body
eat
how
into
these
those
way

Key Words

Look at the pictures.
Read the sentences.

The Luna Moth

1. Look at **those** moths.
2. Look **how** fat the **body** is!
3. Look at those wings on their **backs**.
4. **These** moths do not **eat** bugs.
5. They go this **way** and that way **into** the night.

What do these moths look like?

Phonics Games
NGReach.com

Luna Moths

by Kathryn Mead

Look at this big green bug. It hangs on a stick.

This is a luna moth. It has big wings on its back. Look how big its wings are!

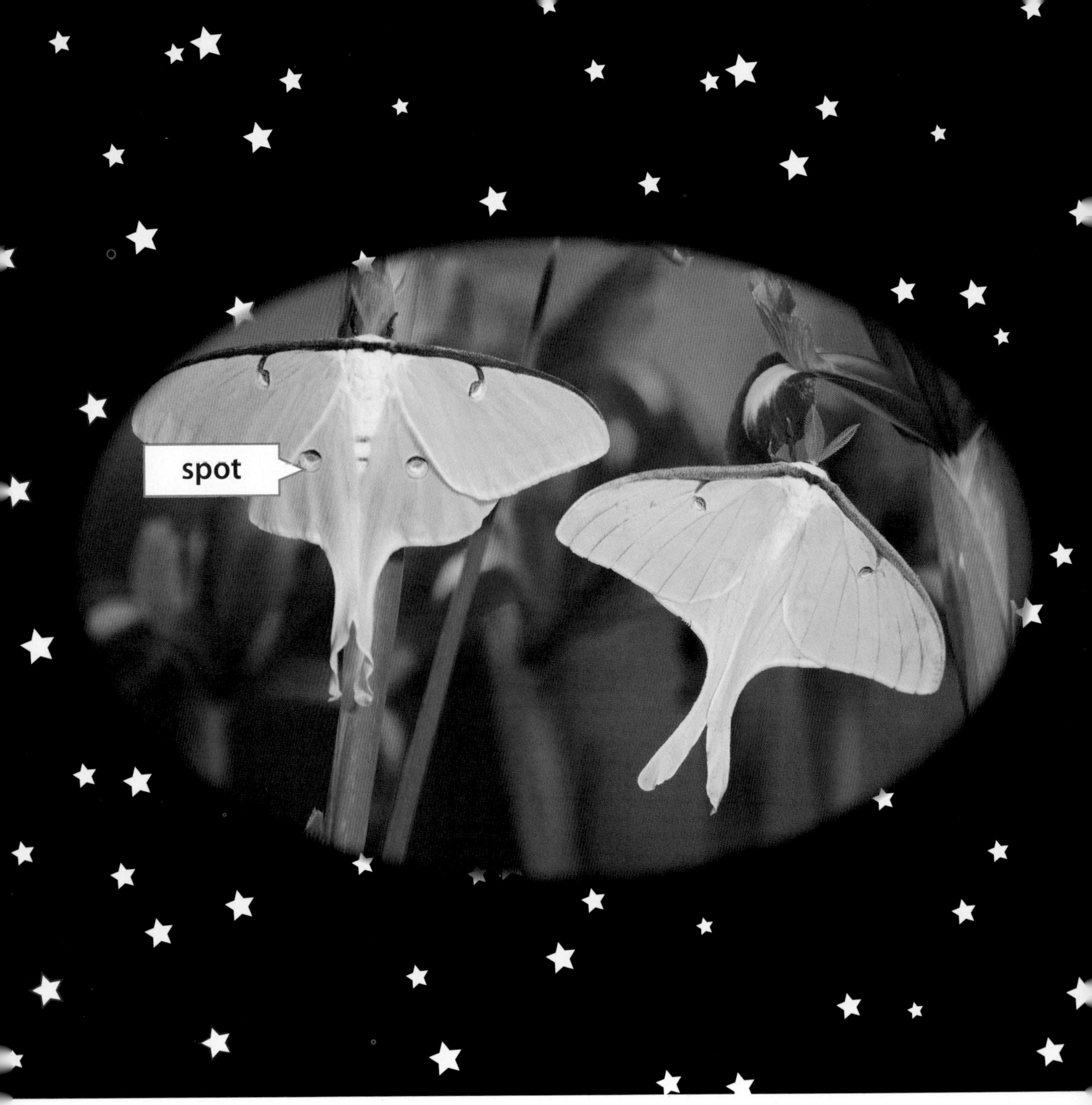

Wings

The wings have spots. If the moth sits still, you can see the spots. But it can slide its wings into its back. Then you can not see the spots.

A moth has a wide wing span. The wings have long, slim tips. Some wings have a red or black stripe.

Body

A moth has a long, fat body. Its body has a lot of fuzz.

It has six legs. Its legs can grab a stem or stick.

Luna Moths Are Night Bugs

Luna moths like the night. You will not find them in the day. What do they do at night?

They spot a stem, stop, and sit. They spring up and flit off. They flutter and scatter this way and that way. But they do *not* eat.

Eggs

Those little blobs are eggs. Moths stop and drop them off at night.

Look at these little bugs with stripes. They will be moths one day.

Look for luna moths at home. Look for those big green wings. If you see them flap, the luna moth is out! ❖

Blends with s

Read these words.

spill	skip	smells	scab	slid
stops	snaps	spins	sniffs	swim

Find words with **s** blends.
Use letters to build them.

s p i l l

Talk Together

Choose words from the box above to tell a partner what you see.

Get Frog Back to Its Tree!

How can frog get back to its tree?
Follow these steps to help it get there.

1. Can you spot a crab with a red body? Go that way.
2. Look for something that stops traffic. Go that way.
3. Find a stack of flapjacks (so good to eat!) and go that way.
4. Look for a black truck. Go that way.
5. Cross a split log.
6. You will run smack into the tree!

Acknowledgments
Grateful acknowledgment is given to the authors, artists, photographers, museums, publishers, and agents for permission to reprint copyrighted material. Every effort has been made to secure the appropriate permission. If any omissions have been made or if corrections are required, please contact the Publisher.

Photographic Credits
CVR (bg) Creatas/Jupiterimages. (inset) Jason L. Price/Shutterstock. **2** (bl) Valentyn Volkov/ iStockphoto. (br) Ashley Pickering/iStockphoto. (cl) Fotocrisis/Shutterstock. (cr) Dwight Nadig/ iStockphoto. (tl) Creatas/Jupiterimages. (tr) Jan Krejci/iStockphoto. **3** Liz Garza Williams/ Hampton-Brown/National Geographic School Publishing. **4** Chun-lin Ho/iStockphoto. **5** (bl) Dave Benisrael/National Geographic Image Collection. (br) christophe fouquin/iStockphoto. (c) Lynsey Allan/Shutterstock. (tl) Value Stock Images/Unlisted Images. (tr) Paul Zahl/National Geographic Image Collection. **6-7** Paul Sutherland/National Geographic Image Collection. **7** (inset) Frank Harrison/ANT Photo Library. **8-9** Michael Durham/Minden Pictures. **10-11** Michael & Patricia Fogden/Minden Pictures. **11** (inset) Kitchin & Hurst/Tom & Pat Leeson. **12** (bl) Subbotina Anna/Shutterstock. (br) Stockbyte/Getty Images. **12-13** (t) Stephen Dalton/Minden Pictures. **13** (b) Creatas/Jupiterimages. **14** Annika Erickson/Blend Images/ age fotostock. **15** (bc) Fritz Rauschenbach/Corbis. (bl) Dirk Ercken/Shutterstock. (br) David Northcott/Danita Delimont Stock Photography. (t) Liz Garza Williams/Hampton-Brown/National Geographic School Publishing. **16** (bl) PhotographerOlympus/iStockphoto. (br) Tim Pannell/ Flame/Corbis. (cl) Oscar Gutierrez/iStockphoto. (cr) Tony Freeman/PhotoEdit. (tl) Laurin Johnson/iStockphoto. (tr) Margaret Sidlosky. **17** Liz Garza Williams/Hampton-Brown/National Geographic School Publishing. **18-19** Leroy Simon/Visuals Unlimited. **20** Darrell Gulin/ Danita Delimont Stock Photography. **21** Clive Varlack. **22** (l) Doug Wechsler/Animals Animals. **22-23** (r) B. Runk/S. Schoenberger/Grant Heilman Photography. **24-25** (l) Maxim Tupikov/ Shutterstock. **25** (r) Raymond Mendez/Animals Animals. **26** Dwight R. Kuhn Photography. **27** Dwight R. Kuhn Photography. **28** Stephen St. John/National Geographic Image Collection. **29** Liz Garza Williams/Hampton-Brown/National Geographic School Publishing.

Illustrator Credits
3, 17, 29, 30-31 Jackie Stafford

National Geographic School Publishing
Hampton-Brown
www.NGSP.com

Printed in the USA.
Quad Graphics, Leominster, MA

ISBN:978-0-7362-8060-0

17 18 19
10 9 8 7 6